Empathy

Also by Mei-mei Berssenbrugge

The Lit Cloud (with Kiki Smith)
Hello, the Roses
I Love Artists: New and Selected Poems
Concordance (with Kiki Smith)
Nest
Four Year Old Girl
Endocrinology (with Kiki Smith)
Sphericity (with Richard Tuttle)
Hiddenness (with Richard Tuttle)
Empathy
The Heat Bird
Random Possession
Summits Move with the Tide

Empathy

MEI-MEI BERSSENBRUGGE

A New Directions Book

Empathy was first published by Station Hill Press in 1989. Revisions have been made for this new edition.

Manufactured in the United States of America
New Directions Books are printed on acid-free paper
First published as a New Directions Paperbook (NDP1468) in 2020
Design by Eileen Bellamy

Library of Congress Cataloging-in-Publication Data
Names: Berssenbrugge, Mei-mei, author.
Title: Empathy / Mei-mei Berssenbrugge.
Description: First New Directions edition. | New York: New Directions Books, 2020. | "A New Directions book."
Identifiers: LCCN 2019047012 | ISBN 9780811229401 (paperback; alk. paper) | ISBN 9780811229418 (ebook)
Subjects: LCGFT: Poetry.
Classification: LCC PS3552.E77 E4 2020 | DDC 811/.54—dc23
LC record available at https://lccn.loc.gov/2019047012

10 9 8 7 6 5 4 3 2 1

New Directions Books are published for James Laughlin
by New Directions Publishing Corporation
80 Eighth Avenue, New York 10011
ndbooks.com

To Leslie Marmon Silko

Contents

I

The Blue Taj

There is your 'dream' and its 'approximation.'
Sometimes the particular attributes of your labyrinth
seem not so ghastly. More often blue shimmering
walls of the house crack with a sudden drop
in temperature at night, or the builder substitutes
cobalt plaster, which won't hold at this exposure.

Your client vetoes a roof garden, often
because of money, or he likes to kiss you at dawn
and you want to sleep late. Sometimes a person
holds out for the flawless beveled edge, but might
end up with something half-built, its inlay
scavenged long ago.

Let a ragged edge between the two be lightning
or falling water, and figure its use: the distance
away of a person poised in the air with wings on.
If you string a rope through a pulley at his waist
at least you can lift the New Zealand ferns.
Any fall will *seem* deliberate.

Tan Tien

As usual, the first gate was modest. It is dilapidated. She can't tell
which bridge crossed the moat, which all cross sand now, disordered with footsteps.
It's a precise overlay of circles on squares, but she has trouble locating
the main avenue, and retraces her steps in intense heat for the correct entrance,
which was intentionally blurred, the way a round arch can give onto a red wall,
far enough in back of the arch for sun to light it.

If being by yourself separates from your symmetry, which is
the axis of your spine in the concrete sense, but becomes a suspension
in your spine like a layer of sand under the paving stones of a courtyard
or on a plain, you have to humbly seek out a person who can listen to you,
on a street crowded with bicycles at night, their bells ringing.

And any stick or straight line in your hand can be your spine,
like a map she is following in French of Tan Tien. She wants space to fall
to each side of her like traction, not weight dispersed within a mirror. At any time,
an echo of what she says will multiply against the walls in balanced,
dizzying jumps like a gyroscope in the heat, but she is alone.

Later, she would remember herself as a carved figure and its shadow on a blank board,
but she is her balancing stick, and the ground to each side of her is its length,
disordered once by an armored car, and once by an urn of flowers at a crossing,
because Tan Tien is a park, now. The stick isn't really the temple's bisection around her,
like solstice or ancestor. This Tang Dynasty peach tree would be a parallel levitation
in the spine of the person recording it.

Slowly the hall looms up. The red stairway's outline gives way to its duration
as it extends and rises at a low angle.
In comparison to the family, the individual hardly counts, but they all
wait for her at a teahouse inside the wall.
First the gold knob, then blue tiers rise above the highest step,
the same color as the sky.

When one person came to gain its confidence,
she imagines he felt symmetry as flight after his fast among seven meteorites
in the dark. He really felt like a globe revolving within a globe.
Even the most singular or indivisible particle or heavenly sphere will adjust
when the axis extending beyond itself is pushed, or the sphere it is within
is pushed. What she thought was her balance flattens into a stylized dragon
on the marble paving stones.

Yet she's reluctant to leave the compound. Only the emperor
could walk its center line. Now, anyone can imagine how it felt
to bring heaven news. She is trying to remember this in Hong Kong
as the tram pulls suddenly above skyscrapers and the harbor
and she flattens against her seat, like a reversal occurring in the poles,
or what she meant by, no one can imagine how.

Alakanuk Break-Up

1

To find out the temperature, she tosses a cup of water into the air.
Will it evaporate before it hits the ground?
She goes outside and tosses a cup of alcohol into the air.
Then she keeps looking into the air.

When her attention is discontinuous, this no longer means that she
is inattentive. In the same way, they can measure the plain, now,
although the plain and the temperature are vacuums her heat sweeps
across, even before she has turned.

When she turns, the ice she had been standing on is changing into
foam and is about to drift away. It rumbles as it is changing.
She watches it recede until it is a slit of light entering the brain,
because the brain is protecting itself against the light.

Here is the event horizon. You can focus on a cone-shaped rock
in the bay. You can make it larger and closer than the ice
surrounding it, because you have the power to coax the target.
This breaks up your settlement in a stretch of infinity.

Then you tie some string to a stick and toss it in front of you,
as you are watching the rock. Then you keep drawing it back.
Sometimes the stick disappears in front of you, until you draw
it back. At these times, the rock becomes yourself

wearing soft bedclothes and with burned eyes.
You balance three horizons. In the same way you press down
on her shoulders and gently push the person into the ground,
which is constantly changing in the current and on the tide.

This is where they have concentrated you. All that time
you had been noting the direction of snowdrifts and stalks bent
in the south wind. Nevertheless, a storm can distract your attention.
Your attention becomes the rasping noise of a stick drawn across
the edge of a bowl at a party. It draws attention tenuously
from your fingers, the way your body starts to hurry in the wind.

This is where they have concentrated you, in order to be afraid
or in order to recreate the line between your mind and your mind
on the other side of a blue crack in the ice, so you can sit
facing each other, like ice floes folded up and cut up
and piled up against each other, and so you know enough to stop
as soon as you lose your direction.

Then, if you are on the ocean, with poor visibility, with no wind
and you cannot be seen, please go around the outside of an ice
floe, because the ocean has dust particles, which will sparkle
and indicate the direction of the sun, she says.

When you look up, you see a heavy frost has formed on the window,
which had been damp for a while each morning, and then would dry
up and crackle. You pass the window. The ice begins to melt
and drops of water travel down the window diagonally, because
of your speed.

You take the window and place it in your mouth, and meanwhile
fishline attached to your red bandanna jiggles in the dark,
because you are losing consciousness. It swarms around the rag
when you look up at it against the sky.

The dashes you had applied so carefully, in order to record rotation
in the sky have been washed away, leaving milky traces of themselves
and of their trails, so your poor map is now a circuit of spirals you
decode into chrysanthemums, on a sleeve moving past cirrus clouds.

You are a blur of speed concentrating on heading in one direction.
It is the bank above you standing still, because you are being
held back. Sometimes in your path you see darkness that looks
like smoke. When you come to the edge of it, you realize you are
already veering away from it. You have to concentrate on the
dotted line of your lane, which is foretold in threes by the light
and ticks like a meter from your looking at them.

Sitting up, you think someone has been splashing water on your clothes.
Picking up a dash, which had been a warm I-beam in your hand,
you arrange them on a board, oblivious to the sky, because
you can conceive of yourself now, moving on the board or behind
the board. A square of the board lights up and becomes the single
headlight of a car, indicating another person.

If the gravity of this moment outweighs your knowledge of where
you are, that is pathetic. That is what makes the space above the
ocean so attractive, but you still know enough to travel in a
straight line through a patch of fog, and continue to walk when
you emerge, with some fog clinging to you, up to your waist.

Each time you forge an off-shoot of the river, you are hoping it
is the river. It is a little mild time. You see a row
of gulls lined up on the ice, their chests puffed toward the sun,
which is the color of apricots on the snow.

You pass a man lying on the snow, moving his head up and down
and singing. At first the monotony of his movement makes it hard
to concentrate on what he is saying. The snow around him has
frozen into patterns of wavy lines, so there are luminous blue
shadows all around you. This is obviously an instrument for his
location which her voice is occupying. It is grating across the
pointed places in the form of vapor trails.

It is so mild, you are beginning to confuse your destination with
your location. Your location is all the planes of the animal
reconstituting itself in front of you.

2

Anyone who is all right would not be coming in covered with fog.

It is a pattern when it is moving. When it is moving collisions
of things that happen produce a wavering but recognizable image
that merges into the ground when it is still. It is a black diamond
that condenses you mentally as it collapses. It is a black diamond
on the ground, and the diamond is moving. Then it disappears
when you look at it, yourself having no coincidence.

The ground is covered with ice.

Many holes in the ice are glowing with light.
You could say one light is a slanting plank that interrupts the ice. It
could be a bridge, except where new ice is closing it off into a small
enclosure like a holding pen or a bed. The human shines through from behind
and below seams and holes in the ice. The human hovers like a mood.
On a molecular level, the human remains, as a delicate glittering accent
on the dateline, like a light flashing upriver, which can only be seen
by the first person who looks on it, because her looking is equivalent
to clocking its velocity in a chute or a tunnel to her.

She considers these the unconscious lessons of a dominant force
that is being born, and as it becomes, its being is received structure.
First ice crystals, then heavier glass obscures the light,
so she walks back and forth talking to herself in a white soundless
sphere past the trash of the village.

She crosses pressure ridges which form a fringe between old ice
and open water. And the ice responds to her haphazard movement.
The snow is moving about the ice, some of it settling, some of it blowing.
She notices certain portions are ice, while others are covered with snow,
which is easy to make tracks on. So she is careful not to step on that snow.

Twenty miles of frozen ridges buckle under snow,
but when she travels under the ice, the ice would be like fog.
Inside the fog is a jail fire. Flames lure a quantity
of what is going to happen to her into equivocalness
by softening her body with heat, as if the house she is in
suddenly rises, because people still want her.

She prefers to lie down like a river, when it is frozen in the valley
and lie still, but bright lines go back and forth
from her mouth, as she vomits salt water.
This is the breakthrough in plane. The plane itself is silent.
Above and behind the plain lies the frozen delta. Above and in
front of her, fog sinks into the horizon, with silence as a material,
so she is walking among formations of rock. Once again, she can make
a rock in a distant wash move closer to her, where it splays out
like contents its occurrence there. Once again, her solitariness
can flow into the present moment, although she seems to know what
is going to happen.

This is an image represented by a line of ice slabs facing a line
of rocks. One rock seems a little heavier and darker than the others,
but for now, they are two lines of tinkling unaccompanied voices.

The rest can be correspondingly inferred, as a line of rocks
leading toward a distant mountain, as into a distorting mirror,
which once again grows darker and denser, crossing over into mass
for a while, before returning to the little saxophone repetition
with which it began, like rubble under her feet.

Still, anything can still happen. She is still unable to distinguish
one wave from another. This is her nervous system attempting
to maintain its sweep across the plain.
Everything is still moving, and everything is still one texture,
altered from sheer space to the texture of a wall.

The route-through tightens around the nervous system like a musculature.

It floats like a black mountain against the night sky, although she will remember
a mountain glimmering with ore. Then it darkens for her return.
The river branches, and the sea has become blank as mirrors each
branch of the river flows into.

3

Sometimes I think my spirit is resting in the darkness of my stomach.
The snow becomes light at the end of winter. The summer
is an interruption of intervals that disappear, like his little dance
before the main dances, a veridical drug.

A wafer of space beneath the ice starts to descend, like
the edge of her sleeve across a camera lens. Pretty soon
the ice will be all broken up. There is no space left. You look
down on a break-up of little clouds over the plain, as if the house
you are in suddenly rises, to relieve the nervous pressure of light.

Twenty miles of frozen ridges become a lace of moss
and puddles too flat to see and which are breathing. Here is
a snowdrift that has begun to melt. Here is an old woman
talking about a young person who is androgynous, across a distortion
of radio waves, trying to locate you. And she is only moving
from her knees down.

The snow becomes light at the end of winter. How ice changes
on either side of the boat is not a tactic. The drum is a boat.
The mail-route is a line of controlled electric light.
They will scatter their clothes anywhere in this light. You leave
your shirt near the snow machine. It is the initial color on the tundra.

Texas

I used the table as a reference and just did things from there
in register, to play a form of feeling out to the end, which is
an air of truth living objects and persons you use take on,
when you set them together in a certain order, conferring privilege
on the individual, who will tend to dissolve if his visual presence
is maintained, into a sensation of meaning, going off by itself.
First the table is the table. In blue light
or in electric light, it has no pathos. Then light separates
from the human content, a violet-colored net or immaterial haze, echoing
the violet iceplant on the windowsill, where he is the trace of a desire.

Such emotions are interruptions in landscape and in logic
brought on by a longing for direct experience, as if her memory of experience
were the trace of herself. Especially now, when things have been flying apart in all directions,
she will consider the hotel lobby the inert state of a form. It is the location
of her appointment. And gray enamel elevator doors are the relational state,
the place behind them being a ground of water or the figure of water. Now,
she turns her camera on them to change her thinking about them into a thought

in Mexico, as the horizon when you are moving can oppose the horizon inside
the elevator via a blue Cadillac into a long tracking shot. You linger
over your hand at the table. The light becomes a gold wing on the table. She sees
it opening, with an environment inside that is plastic and infinite,
but is a style that has got the future wrong.

Duration of Water

So that I make you a microcosm or symbolic center of the public
like a theatre, with hundreds of painted scenes combining and recombining
in order to exaggerate situations of joy or pain on stage, instead of
five short songs about you, accompanying dancers who seem to float on their backs
in still water, as the empyrean. They would be the water motor. Three stones
protrude from the water, and three instruments combine and repeat a simple scale,
but some passions only resolve with fire and weather catastrophes.
The orchestra nevertheless clears like foliage
for Yang Kuei-Fei's sigh, when she hears the emperor wants her.
There is a red line on the boards I can follow in the thick smoke
or mist. The shoulders of the man change scale, as if I had
been manipulating the field inside a small box, to see how light
can transform me into foliage, as a sexual punishment. The music
can take on the cold or heat of the air like blue chameleons on the limbs of the tree,
as if you could look through leaves into the empyrean. I can turn back
my sleeve with the multiplicity of detail of the battleground. The colors
combine into legible hues at a distance. There is a craft at work
to reconcile emotion in a purely speculative ambience,
tracking the last aria, like a duration of water
which is a piece of white silk.

The Star Field

Placing our emotion on a field, I said, became a nucleus of space,
defined by a rain of light and indeterminate contours of a landscape,
like the photograph of an explosion, and gave the travel of your gaze into it, or on me,
imaginative weight of the passage along a gulf of space
or a series of aluminum poles.

She walks through rooms of blue chain-linked fence, a spacious tennis court
of rooms on concrete, instead of the single movement of a room, where sky and earth
would come together.

Outside is the field she is thinking about: a category of gray dots
on a television screen of star data, representing no one's experience,
but which thrills all who gaze on it, so it must be experience. And
the land at large becomes the light on the land.

A coyote or a flicker's call
is transfixed at the moment before its dissemination across the field,
a sediment of, instead
of the trace of feeling, the ratio of people to the space.
I pass through blue focal planes, a scene of desire.

The material of the sky adjacent to me eludes me, a pure signifier
shifting sense, the sky or space a gradation of material, the light
a trace of mobility like a trace of light on a sensitive screen,
extended into the plane of the trace
and marked by light poles or drawn close by a planet at the edge.

Your name becomes a trace of light. Through
its repetition and deferral, my life protects itself
from blurs, time-lapses, flares
of the sexual act, its mobility of an afterimage.

Then I can understand the eye's passage into depth
as an inability to stand still for you to see.

Chinese Space

First there is the gate from the street, then some flowers inside the wall,
then the inner, roofed gate. It is a very plain wall, without expressionistic means,
such as contrasting light on paving stones inside the courtyard to the calligraphed foundation stones.
My grandfather called this the façade or Baroque experience, rendering a courtyard transparent.
The eye expecting to confront static space experiences a lavish range of optical events,
such as crickets in Ming jars, their syncopation like the right, then left, then right progress
into the house, an experience that cannot be sustained in consciousness, because
your movement itself binds passing time, more than entering directs it.

A red door lies on a golden mirror with the fascinating solidity and peacefulness of the pond
in the courtyard, a featureless space of infinite depth where neither unwanted spirits nor light
could enter directly from outside. It lies within the equally whole space of the yard,
the way we surrounded our individuals, surrounded by a house we could not wholly
retain in memory. Walking from the inner gate across a bridge which crossed four ways
over the carp moat, turning right before the ice rink, we pass roses imported from Boston,
and enter the main courtyard, an open structure like a ruin. This is not remembering,
but thinking its presence around eccentric details such as a blue and white urn turned up to dry,
although certain brightnesses contain space, the way white slipcovered chairs with blue seams
contain it.

The potential of becoming great of the space is proportional to its distance away from us,
a negative perspective, the way the far corner of the pond becomes a corner again as we approach
on the diagonal, which had been a vanishing point. The grandmother poses beside rose bushes.
That is to say, a weary and perplexing quality of rough wall behind her gives a power of tolerance
beyond the margins of the photograph. Space without expansion, compactness without restriction
make this peculiar and intense account of the separable person from her place in time,

although many families live in the partitioned house now. The reflecting surface of the pond
should theoretically manifest too many beings to claim her particular status in the space,
such as a tiger skin in space.

After the house was electrically wired in the thirties, he installed a ticker tape machine connected
to the American Stock Exchange. Any existence occupies time, he would say in the Chinese version,
reading stock quotations and meaning the simplicity of the courtyard into a lavish biosphere,
elevating the fact of its placement to one of our occupation of it, including the macaw speaking Chinese,
stones representing infinity in the garden. This is how the world appears when the person
becomes sufficient, i.e., like home, an alternation of fatigue and relief in the flexible shade of date trees,
making the house part of a channel in space, which had been interior, with mundane fixtures
as on elevator doors in a hotel, a standing ashtray that is black and white.
The family poses in front of the hotel, both self-knowing and knowing others at the same time.
This is so, because human memory as a part of unfinished nature is provided
for the experience of your unfinished existence.

II

Jealousy

Attention was commanded through a simple, unadorned, unexplained, often decentered presence,
up to now, a margin of empty space like water, its surface contracting, then melting
along buried pipelines, where gulls gather in euphoric buoyancy. Now,
the growth of size is vital, the significance of contraction by a moat, a flowerbed, or
a fenced path around the reservoir, its ability to induce the mind's growing experience of the breadth
and depth of physical association, which turns out to be both vital and insufficient, because
nature never provides a border for us, of infinite elements irregularly but flexibly integrated,
like the rhythm between fatigue and relief of accommodation, or like a large apartment. Now,
the construction is not the structure of your making love to me. The size of your body on mine
does not equal your weight or buoyancy, like fireworks on a television screen, or the way
an absent double expresses inaccuracy between what exists and does not exist in the room
of particular shape, volume, etc., minute areas and inferred lines we are talking about.
You have made a vow to a woman not to sleep with me. For me, it seemed enough
that love was a spiritual exercise in physical form and what was seen is what it was,
looking down from the twelfth floor, our arms resting on pillows on the windowsill. It is midnight.
Fireworks reflecting in the reservoir burst simultaneously on the south and the north shores,
so we keep turning our heads quickly to see both starry spheres, instead of
a tangible, and an intangible event that does not reflect. Certain definite brightness
contains spaciousness. A starry night, like a fully reflecting surface, claims
no particular status in space, or being of its own.

Recitative

Her voice on the telephone, while she is out of town performing the activities she is describing,
but with a poignant elevation of mood, is quantifiably precise, insistently formal,
as stripped down as a Palladian animation of form. Her beauty is identified with order,
liveliness, serenity, a courtly arrangement of platforms or painted stars.
Half their conversation is in shadow, so they speak in and out of a diagonal wedge of light.
The possibility of static or a gap on a starry electric night gives the impression of her body
constantly engaged in transition, but she desires to enter a body of material by talking.

In Sumer and in Egypt in the 3rd millennium B.C., words were spoken like an arrangement of stars,
an orderly procession of luminous beings, who counted poetry with sound,
until speaking gave way to a duration that would not reconstitute, so she may appear
as a large masklike close-up and as an immobile figure in white on the bed,
who actually absorbs space.

One can paint stars on a black lead background,
equivocal stars casting carpets of desire here and there in the middle of an errand,
which up to then had proceeded in the state of non-imploring urgency of a body in diagonal,
an image of outreach or hailing. For me, it seemed that love was a spiritual exercise in physical form,
and the diagonal was glints off an inferred line of sun lingering, as spring
synchronized with the double space of her desire and her desire for their presence
to be hieratic, not wholly expressive, a standard of grace in the corridor of a day,
with narcissus. If it is through counting that speech is connected to time,
then crossing an inferred estuary of this conversation is a rest in music.

The Carmelites

Like the camera, memory is a device and feeling is a device, or a souvenir.
The interior of the courtyard lights up. Its doorway becomes a luminous square in the dark,
and I can regulate the rate at which a blue wooden bench passes across it, like a car,
or returns, when I back up. An apple tree in blossom in the courtyard travels across the screen.
There was some light at the edge of a flowering branch of a density that could be almost a scratch into the day.
It moves across the courtyard in a light that seems unspecified, as through a lens opened in the dark
for a long time, so the stasis of a doorway itself conveys immanence. Experience of it
is the result of a deepening relation to the light, regressing from conscious recognition
to a remembered involvement between so many minor cycles of sleep and waking, just as
your silence begins to look like so many examples of experience. Now, the sublime is the interval
of the exposure, the way silence once signified but no longer signifies the limits of discourse,
sabotaging instructive strategies of the film and the garden, in which we are audience or the wall.
Not as in a Chinese garden.

Apple trees bloom haphazard in the field around the nunnery.
The atmosphere in daylight poses questions about passing light more difficult than those
the ordinary person in nature, for whom the horizon and amount of light define the limits of intensity,
has long since dissolved into a sense of spaciousness for things to take place.
As he or she begins to walk among the trees, each tree would be part of a ceiling consisting
of so many sunk or hollowed out compartments for the silence. For me,
the blossoms became numerous edges of the volume of each tree, soft, or a missing part
in its openness, the way an exposed nest is upturned that should be concealed in leaves,
or your voice that is so emotionally distant.

The Margin

A sense of being responsible for a crisis may also give a feeling of control. Victims
prefer to accept the guilt blame entails to admitting that life is unfair,
a curtain of air as its margin of yielding for the sake of her emotion. The way a peach-colored
amaryllis can cut up the space of a room, depending on how he places it in the room, an environment erodes.
An invisible plane of air is almost undetectable to touch as you walk down into the canyon,
laden with hue. It moves horizontally along the crestline, but varies vertically in temperature,
making a complex profile in cold shade from where I look onto the illuminated planes of a far cliff.

The air seems very complicated to sense or very subtle, because it is very difficult to relate
to a particular pleasure or pain. This is because so much imagination is involved.
Instead of the situation of rock climbing or making love, bringing a person into the present,
unobstructed space is very provocative, because it is ubiquitous. It seeks to express a wall,
rather than be contained within or dependent on the wall as a separated object, or a stratigraphic series
around a branching weed, or the memory of snowing for half an hour in it.

A crestline is red, but the lower wall and I are in blue shadow,
because of the implication of gravity holding air around the amaryllis, and versus
the weightlessness of light on selected cliff faces complexly structured into lines and cords
as an experience of one version of the body. A belief in personal invulnerability to caprice
disintegrates slowly with the pulls and weights of the body in motion,
whereas unobstructed space is very, very plain. Although

no site is transferable, images of a site become more and more abstract through color.
They also charge with fiction when revealed as shot from the point of view of a couple
in a helicopter, a surveillance of peach-colored snow on volcanic ash, seeming static figures.

Then the strip surprises you by changing or seeming to change ever so slightly
in the shadow of the mountain. You see a broad luminous horizon of desert
in the distance, an allusive expanse of expanded, indifferent purity.
Because your eye clings to this margin, it appears to speed up.

Naturalism

1

He calls it instincts and their vicissitudes, or emotions, at the border
in blue and white. The river ice moves down the open channel of the river
or it moves up the river. It is a disheveled stripe of ice moving past
ice piled on the bank, like a filmstrip along the lens of ice, and
it seems most personal when the tide changes, across forty-five minutes, almost indiscernibly,
so that the mode of my feeling was taken care of simply by the demands of observing it.
The overcast goes into patches of blue and the clouds whiten,
as if television cameras were suspended above and reflected in the water,
which takes on a sheen of aluminum in bright sun.

2

A feeling moves like a hand across the blue and white mountain range in bright sun, after
a plain of little white clouds breaks up. The agitation of personal experience
was thought to becloud its intellectual content,
when the mode of an act could be taken care of simply by the demands of the feeling-at-hand's
attempt to unify the meaning of discontinuous affections,
formally allusive to plains for unity. My feeling was not mystical but conjectural.
Its naturalism is an authentic source of pathos, delicate and precise,
but it is not good manners to him.

3

A live bird joins the flock of birds across the bay, the flock
in soft focus behind the windowpanes of snow, stars, or flowers.
How an emotion grew out of or failed to grow out of the landscape
was the most important determinant of the ties it later formed with him,
an attempt to wrest from the landscape itself what others got from relations,
its performance of innate or unconscious dexterity. Wind became a symbol
for resistance of the thing being depicted to its depiction, or conventionalization
into the pathos of good manners.

4

I have to communicate to you the possibilities of fantasy, the possibility that the real world
could be different from the apparent. But I have no confidence. Only
an erotic concentration on a vicissitude of light,
so the visual part is a mirage
for my memory of the landscape. The image of reality and mirage are mixed, so you see *through*,
under the control of the camera with my arm and my emotion.

5

The while is long with the speed of time. It is a camera controlled by the participant,
so the speed and the time control the image, too. The feeling is the afterimage of yourself
you are always coming to, so I like landscape where coming to the feeling
is always elemental or hierarchical. Or,
if camera sounds too harsh or formal for this elusive process, we can just say, we
grasp an imaginative continuity that corresponds to the landscape,
creating an emotion greater than what can be accounted for
by its blue and white plains.

6

What can be at stake with an emotion is not a location and its occupation,
but the capacity to move more or less at will. The coast's use of feedback can steady
and bring into unison several stages of the motion with great elegance.
My own experience of it ranged from the therapeutic to a more constrained, task-oriented
intuition. This is a direct effect of my empathic involvement,
a persistent, attentive involvement with you,
although it is impossible to control the body as the object.
You can remember how the far grass on a sandbar lit up, as at the end of an afternoon lightning
storm on a foreground range of waves. When
I walked before the waves, they were pierced by a row of light at a low level, like footlights.

7

I had continued in a state of exhaustion, until a control channel broke down,
but the exhaustion is reversible,
as when a video camera is a quartz stone on a plane of mica
in sunlight so bright it becomes silence.
There is no outside communication, and you think I have gone over the edge. I had
a sort of nostalgia about it. In the same sense that the emotion was too vehement in the beginning,
I had this nostalgia, this deep regret at having to return to normal, but
I could do nothing to prolong or shorten it.

Fog

1

Hundreds of millions of years ago, days were many hours shorter.

All things, sounds, stories, and beings were related, and this complexity was obvious. It was not simplified by ideas of relationship in one person's mind.

Paths of energy were forced to stay in the present moment by being free of references, making it impossible to focus on two things at once, and showing by its quietness that energy of attention is as much a source of value and of turbulence as energy of emotion.

As lava burst from the ground to cover the planet, it also freed water, which escaped as massive, billowing fog, a contradicting ambition of consciousness to acquire impressions and retain strong feelings.

Fog is a kind of grounded cloud composed like any cloud of tiny drops of water or of ice particles, forming an ice fog.

Since water is 800 times denser than air, investigators were long puzzled as to why fogs did not quickly disappear through fallout of water particles to the ground.

It turns out that the drops do fall, but in fog creating conditions, they are buoyed up by rising currents or they are continually replaced by new drops condensing from water vapor in the air.

Their realism is enhanced by smoothing away, or ignoring discontinuities in the fog, for images of what we really see when we travel. Beautiful, unrepeatable, fleeting impressions can be framed only within the contradicting ambition of her consciousness to acquire impressions and to retain her feeling, a way of repeating a dream.

Large areas of the sky change from totally transparent to nearly opaque within a few minutes, although throughout a lifetime, the night sky appears remarkably constant.

Showing what they are without revealing what they are, paths of energy are transformed at the moment before their dissemination into an empty field, like dew you see on a spider web when the sun hits it, after there were spiders.

2

There is a great wall in the fog and rain.

There are some mountains in the mist.

There is the line of a wall in the mist. I go in and out of the fog on the rim trail, and the mountains rise in fog among yellow leaves.

There is a veil of fog between her and a sunlit flank of yellow leaves.

Slow-whirling galaxies allow stars and gas to fall into hot disks of matter, orbiting around massive holes at the centers of the galaxies, allowing a branch to spring up at the moment when snow melts from it.

Your concentration is interrupted by a shadow on the periphery of your memory of her.

Your concentration is a large array, where debris in the mind appears as an intense shower of heat radiation, like a cluster of instincts to the body.

3

As far as the transparency or relative compression of her boundaries is concerned, and your backward focus to it:

A white glass of water is hard to conceive of, because we cannot depict how the same thing would be white and clear, and how this would look. She doesn't know what description these words demand of her, since she is alone.

She can sometimes see the events of a story as if they lay behind a screen, and it were transparent, rather like a sheet of glass, since human beings can be reflected on a smooth white surface in such a way that their reflections seem to lie behind the surface, and are seen through it.

4

She can describe for you the phenomenon of feeling her way through the fog. For whom does she describe this?

What ignorance can her description eliminate?

Which person is supposed to understand her description, people who have been lost in fog before, or people who have lived on the desert and never seen what she would describe?

You can be trying to connect the experience of being lost with something external or physical, but we are really connecting what is experienced with what is experienced.

So, when she tries to talk about the appearance of the people's feelings around her, she wants to connect how it appears to her with what is solid around her, but

she could connect appearance with appearance, how people *seem* to feel, and their communicating with each other within this appearance, from one person to another.

Is it possible for four different people in this way to have four different spatial concepts within the crowd? Somewhat different ones? Different with respect to one or another feature or heat inside a building, such as arm span or eye contact, and that could impair their mutual understanding to a greater or lesser degree? But often hardly at all, like ice broken up on the sea.

From above, I can't tell what distance away it is.

5

It has no shape or color that is stable, as if I had fallen asleep and a long bridge appeared, where my relatives are like companions crossing a bridge.

Her friends and family are like people you meet at the marketplace.

When you look at your husband, you think of a floating flag of the roof.

Even though he is your husband, he is not stable. Anyone believes what anyone says about you.

This is a realm or field in which other people exist in subtler forms than the body in daylight. A part of the person can become visible at a time, or parts of the people, and other parts rest in folds of the fog, as if they were muffled sounds.

It would be hard for you to believe anything within the cloud exists.

His body, which you do not see exists, having dissolved its cells into a body of a cloud, which shifts in and out of focus.

It would not decay.

The body is the space of the point of a moment in your seeing him or hearing him.

You can calm yourself by moving toward one of these points, the way you move along your own breath.

6

You could try to make some fog into a piece of white cloth. This is impossible. Though it is visible, it is not a concrete substance. She tried to make a delicate sound into a cloth. She could not, so that is why he is staying here.

Or, she could alternate dissolving in the light with dissolving in the dark, for speed.

At night, she could see if the country were illuminated, as if it were day. She could see each person's face clearly, and she could remember if she had ever known this person before.

Dreams cannot disturb the fog or you, because your environment has no territory. There is no territory in a fog environment.

7

Lack of clarity within your environment is tormenting. It is felt as shameful. We feel we do not know how to even out a place for ourselves, where we should know our way about. But we get along very well inside buildings, without these distinctions, and without knowing our way about the decrepit structures.

In any serious interaction between them, not knowing your way about extends to the essence of what is between them. What can appear emotional is caused by the emission of energy out of her body, which you feel, but there is also such a thing as "feeling something as luminous,"

thinking of him as the color of polished silver or nickel, or a scratch in these metals.

8

The fog in space and light and dark is analogous to the solid ice of a very pure environment, and how it cracks with water, from one stage to another.

Its area of wide space varies in lightness from place to place, but does it look foggy to her in the darker places? The shadow that a cloud casts is in part darker. She sees the parts of the space that are farther away from the light as darker, but still white, even though she would have to add black to depict it.

Looking around in her room or any wide space in the evening, she can hardly distinguish among the people around her, and now becomes physically frightened of them.

And now, illuminate the space and describe each one you saw in the mist.

There are pictures of dreams in rooms in semi-darkness, but how can she compare the people in these pictures to those she saw in semi-darkness?

9

Bright light slows the senses. A picture of the space in bright light, as if etched by a laser, can slow your sense.

When we see or experience something with the senses and the senses get slowed, we can stop at this object, for example, a person who is beautiful.

As soon as we see this person, perception is blocked by the desire to go toward the person, with the misunderstanding of fog as thought, that just runs on and on. Her awareness is completely lost in distracting clearings of space.

10

The sky, which illuminates everything we see, can be gray. This can be true of someone around you in your family. How can she tell merely by its or his appearance that gray isn't itself luminous?

Thinking of him as the color of polished silver or other metal.

The fog of the way we feel our way into this focus, seeking by feeling, lies in the indefiniteness of the concept of continuing focus, or distance and closeness, that is, of our methods of comparing densities between human beings.

Is foggy that which conceals forms? And does fogginess conceal forms because it obliterates light and shadow, the way light obliterates or shadow obliterates, also?

Black does, but fog doesn't necessarily take away the luminosity of a color.

Darkness is not called a color.

11

The first solution that occurs to us for the problem of the appearance of another person is that ideas of actual feeling, instead of the appearance of feeling refer to points of tiny intervals or patches in the other person.

How are we to compare the feelings between two such intervals, simply by letting one's memory move from one to the other? If you do this to me, if you remember me, how do we know this feeling has not changed in the process? If you do remember correctly, how can we compare the feeling without being influenced by what has happened since?

The way we call a complex of intervals with which you depict the family member, his emotion with respect to you. As if the person were a piece of rose-colored glass.

Would he have the same emotion in a crowd as a piece of rose-colored paper?

A storyline develops based on your moving from one breath to another, and you start to want to continue it, like a span of good health or exceptional beauty. You want to continue it forever, and your memory gets involved, in how you perceive space around you and the human beings or descendants in the space.

You will eventually feel so empty inside, among your family and in your memory of your family, that even while you continue breathing, your breath will not bring volume or space into your lungs.

12

They counted her more accurate and more inaccurate memories as black and white stones.

The more accurate memories turned out to be white on the outside, but they were unconditioned by the desire to form story out of her memory, continuing story, the way we wish this space and light to continue.

Therefore, we appreciate fog, as the power to make a space continue beyond the single perception, into raw material or youth of the body, like a body of light.

It dissolves now at the top of her head, now five lights into her heart. Now, it dissolves into her body. Her friends dissolve into light. They dissolve into her family, which seems to dissolve into clouds that were already full of light.

It is not so much the quality or brightness of light, or her understanding of this light, as the number of times she dissolves. The faster she can dissolve into the space, the better.

It is almost as if the complete dark would be ideal.

III

War Insurance

1

To communicate skillfully, a person must be aware of interpersonal distance, a sense of
whether he or she should reach out or whether he or she should wait. This
kind of distance can become very distorted, so communication is handled unskillfully,
for instance with hatred that finds emphasis through passion. The basic quality
is hatred, but it develops in terms of passion,
the way consciousness is a sort of basic psychological background where the potential of consciousness
is present, like clusters of tiny shreds of felt overlapping large rectangles of felt. They
call attention to the junctures of discontinuous but related layers of need in time
before his or her presence as a matter of subject is transformed
into his or her presence as a matter in space and time, that is, form. Because
there's no way he or she can jump from anything continuous, such as a line, to anything discrete,
such as points, both continuous and discontinuous are real, or models
as near to reality as we get, due to a kind of fundamental ignoring oneself.
Yet, even the model has progressed beyond simultaneous continuity and discontinuity
to a picture of simultaneous presence and absence.
It inspires a consciousness that is formless and floats in an area more vast
and open than the historical,
where anger like love has a potent capacity for neutral energy
that goes along with it, goes, or says.

Each quantum oscillation of his or her clinging to her or him
is a space-like superluminal transfer of order. Nevertheless,
there's an instant change in the coherent structure between their two areas,
a heat inequality of an emergent order, the way separation is

one level of ordering how the model of separation is beginning to be connected to that of knowledge.
Personal interest and a priori erotic attachment led to a form of critical super-alignment,
a lot of innuendo from relatively simple means,
since abstraction occurs in all forms of communication. It is never focused on.
It is difficult to grasp, because we continue to look for something.
He or she moves from vanishing point to vanishing point inside a series of illusions and must attempt
to project him or herself backward into the mass audience,
when the mass audience will acquire new spaciousness for them.
Why does she respond?
Why does his response continue to build on itself?
What is so mysteriously affecting?

2

I am almost always within what has happened to you and must re-perform it in order to move through it,
where paths of measure turn into segments of lines of perspective
and space turns into a projection of itself, like dreaming about dreams,
first from a single, then from multiple vantage points of the audience. Instead of vanishing
in the dark, a spoken line passes behind layers the borders of which
cannot be perceived, of spacious intuition, as on a ricocheting surface of felt. Thus,
when mind considers the problem of him and her as a relation between meaning and language,
this brings to mind the problem that language is the most formless means of what he or she is expressing
and then making transparent with abstractions, such as in the phenomenal moment or with coincidence,
because everything can be told from the present moment. Its sort of transparent experience
begins to develop in which things are really precise without depending on each other.
In this way she takes the principles of abstraction, founded on sight, and applies them to language.
When she does this, a non-visual abstraction occurs, sometimes with the naturalistic edge

of a story that is dissembled by the introduction of her own movements or sounds
as through a corridor of participants or minutes, which is a very pleasant place to begin with,
just to walk.

3

His or her occasional unavailability drew the limits of rationality to experience,
a particular type of person to a particular type of mania,
until the feeling between them possessed the shiniest possible surface and the shiniest possible depth,
as if spontaneously generated out of simple commercial luck, but which moved into divination.
When you play this back, you will be in a different situation
in which fellow-feeling is something realistic, but flashes of it happen constantly.
Why should a paradigm be called a revolution?
Handwriting that is large refers to a place other than in him or her or in the audience.
The light from the side is much more beautiful, because it is less glaring,
when he or she can identify outwardly with the present feeling, a sky tactic,
so there is no center, but the fringe or inference of light, everywhere.

Empathy

1

For me, the insignificant or everyday gesture constructs a choreography of parts
and what touches me is where the inarticulate, the error or tension finds concrete manifestation
and is recognized.

—Beverly Dahlen

First, I see roses in the dark with him, a compaction of spare light,
then a road through the woods in pitch dark. How she perceives the corridor in the dark
is a space within the time in which they were moving,
as if perspective of a space in the dark constructed a hierarchy in her mind,
in reverse of how the contents of her wishes remain unchanged and timeless,
so the innermost nature of her wishes is as much known and unknown to them as the reality of the
 external world.
It is as incompletely presented by what she can see as is the external world
by communication with someone she wishes for.

In this way her interrogation of him appears instead as a dialogue pertaining to uses of power,
because she can only remember what has been consciously said to her,
so that her feeling of identifying with him is like a quick flash or a signal.
When it is intense, tormenting and continuous, it's using itself to construct a rhetorical story again.
This state of confusion is never made comprehensible by being given a plot,
in the same way a complicated plot is only further complicated by being simplified,
although connectedness may not always be an artifice,

for example, when it reveals ways in which she construes what she perceives
according to an internal connection which will announce its conflict in the plot,
a tension like his mistaken gesture, interesting as a site of power formation.
It may well be where the feeling of mysteriousness occurs
in which she believes him, but she doesn't want to prove it,
because an appearance in the dark will not deceive after enough appearances
and everywhere, sooner or later, there will be a hint of a tree or space above a lake,
so describing something as it is could by precise reference gain a neutral tone,
but in this case adheres to his and her manner of asking
where is the space, instead of what space it is.
There occurs an interval of northern lights over their walk, whose circumference is inferable,
but whose outermost region lacks any known form of registration,
such as before that and before that.

2

In an empty stadium they alternate the refrain of a song in Japanese. The light is harsh
on rows of seats like cells of a honeycomb under high magnification.
The entire stadium resembles a honeycomb or geodesic dome turned inside out and concave.
He is saying, I am here. She is saying, where are you.
Speech and thought arise simultaneously as an hysterical question. An idea is a wish.
As a descriptive stream or spontaneous reaction to him,
speech serves as a starting point for uncovering a story through translation from wish into desire,
but when thought becomes reflective, a problem of interpretation enters the stream of emotion itself.
The speaking becomes fixed, although there is no such thing as repetition.

The speaking is a constant notation of parallel streams of thought and observations
whose substance is being questioned in a kind of oral thought at once open and precise,
but with a tension between ideas and her sense of scandal at invoking a real person.
He makes a rift or glimpse, both generative and relative to the glimpse,
a liberty of interruption, or exclusion, inside the stadium
in light so bright she sees her eyelash as a golden line reflecting on the inside of her sunglasses.
In the same way a song must never be allowed to threaten the presentation of what takes place in the song,
so that she may try to develop empathy for what she really wants to happen to her,
instead of desire being the song.

3

Anything with limits can be imagined, correctly or incorrectly, as an object,
even some language in the way that it is remembered, if you consider
each repetition a fact or object of varying strength in various situations of frequency and quantity,
and although you can never vary an unconscious wish,
which can only reveal itself in the contingency of the words, sexualizing the words,
the way a shadow moves up a wall of trees growing intensely gold at sunset.
Her equivalent for this is a time-lapse photograph of lightning, in proportion
to each moment you are looking. It is her attempt to show him a lightning storm
or any interval of colored light on the plain as what is good in life, the person and what is good,
so instead of saying what time it is, she is asking, where is the time, its ratio of an opened lens
on clear sky. It may be relevant to ask if this kind of autobiography limits formal
or object possibilities, meaning less neutral or less real within her empathy for what is good in life
from his point of view. From her point of view, feminizing an art of presence
such as moving or speaking, with its distinct kind of maneuverability,
is akin to those collages that verge on trompe l'oeil. Only when she looks closely

does she realize that that head is really not the one connected to that body, although everyday gestures or tensions accrete an intimacy she can recognize. Be that as it may, real and constant luminosity of the parts can create a real self who will remain forever in the emotion of a necessary or real person. To deny this is to deny the struggle to make certain meanings stick.

The Swan

He calls it their stage, which echoes our first misrecognition of unity. Instances
of false unity he calls the imaginary, and he locates in them sites of her dreams,
out of which she is able to want him. The way stage lighting can be a story by itself, now
she makes time for a story, not coming from her or her coming from her story, but both from before,
seeing a flock of birds fly up from a frozen pond, while you stand in the wind, instead
of hearing wind about to arrive across a huge space, so that her train passes a lagoon
in Connecticut, *and* she sees swans swimming at the edge of ice piled against the shore, feminine swans.
Remembering what I heard you say and fixing my desire for you simultaneously, a meaning
of instability, not hesitance, holds you *and* the swans accountable for making the desire,
although the meaning of the desire existed prior to being desired.

Truth effects produced within a dream, neither true nor false in themselves,
operate through repetition to convey an illusion of truth or meaning,
which may be the constant sum of varying systems of dreams, like birds startling from a cottonwood tree
and wind about to arrive, or your seemingly high standards for truth, considering where
femininity is concerned, similar effects yield various meanings, as when a woman photographed
on two separate occasions on the street at random by a famous photographer, who's dead now,
still finds herself in a purely theoretical relationship with herself in relation to him,
which he refuses to merge with the intermediacy of real light. That immaterial matter truly
leaves objects their own places, lighting and illuminating them. Therefore,

she pays attention to absurd and trivial details where her desire dissolved, among
all sorts of things that happened, both in the present and in general, so her focus on absurdity appears
to be a spontaneous part of the desire itself, where coincidence and nonsense merge in a lover,
until the sky would look on you as a composite of video monitors on surfaces slowly disintegrating
into ice swans which resemble, for example, an opera house.

Finally, one must sort of drop one's reserve, which could be a kind of definition
of physical beauty, without which no transformation takes place, such as
if you were a mother, the interval between the child and you. This is analogous
to her own physical beauty. It dominates, but does not determine its own content
or its experience, because the dream was not a concept but a means of generating experience,
so that the mother and I desire, but the child is a desire, in spite of the child being physical.

A flock of birds flying up acquires the shape of her arcs across the ice, a mirror stage,
echoing our first misrecognition or the imaginary, to look again and then look,
so that if he says or she says, my dream about you is older than my knowing you,
does that mean the dream was dreamed before your meeting him or her?
The meaning of the dream existed prior to the dream, and then I met you and then I dreamt about you,
gratifying an enigma that was solved and then posed, with a resulting fullness
in the dreamer, as with a child to replace himself or replace herself, or as verisimilitude on stage.
Its story is light that moves from cue to cue as over ground.
It resembles an arm reaching out to defend you at a sudden stop, but is rhetorical,
the way your arms full of white down inscribe an immense volume above the ice.

Forms of Politeness

1

Taking advantage of the relationships and interaction which actually exist between what happens
to her and her desire, she creates some metaphors both obvious and opaque, as screens of rays crisscrossing
the landscape in which herself and what she expected from you in the way of support coincide,
so that I and you resemble each other, now. The way they light the land like infrared without a trace
on film, really, part of your image was linked so closely to my desire, it remained inside my body.
It never reached the emotions, which tend to damage the body, but which memory requires.
Thus a formal device was discovered for detailing information that was intimate and largely unacceptable
to what I thought I required from you, regarding beauty in idea and form. She expected distress
to automatically bring about this beauty, like a woman's theft of fire rope from your house,
but not her hanging in the orchard by the house. She was a stranger to you.
She was never in your consciousness. Hence she was never forgotten.
She is in you the way direct experience generates consciousness, adding the energy of its materialization.

To live another person's biography is not the same as to live his or her life.
She constructs a story-line or cluster of anecdotal details, like clothes around the body,
instruments of both defense and expansion, which give meaning to fluctuations, such as in pleasures
occurring between herself and you. Her sunglasses swathed in feathers express
the contingency of a light and a space, so that the anecdote of a hanging could be utilized
as colorist or combinatory data, instead of her instinct for the imaginary in which what she imagines
represents what happens, whether or not it misrepresents it.

Sometimes it happens during a routine she represents by evenness of light on the land
or when things usually mean nothing, like harmony in light, what happens and something to mean
join accidentally. The thing isn't what it is, but it is like what it is.

Like a fake, it doesn't mean anything, although there is something to mean,
so that her solitude is the guise of unending repetition of a hanging or her relationship with you,
in which all that is to be included will find a place. This is empathy or sharing her intuition with her.
You look into someone's eyes as if you were seeing through the face.

2

Because it's not possible to absorb more than one insight at a time,
there seems to be a contradiction between the visual or space, and the context or meaning.
She felt deep uneasiness with the image of this sunset of unnatural energy, its sinister expression
of an order of impossible beauty we thought we lost, accounting for the intensity of yellow light on the hill,
which is not a thing, *and* it is not a metaphor, the way your life is not a metaphor to her, or
the way intense light on the hill is a recollection *en plein air*, in the sense that it happened.
Soon the background turns gray and the hill regains its natural color, but there are three dimensions of gray.
This is a metaphor for the fact that the hanged woman actually made contact with you, although you never
    knew her.

There is a link with her appearance, as with sex, or the way a name is attached to something
after naming it, by the occurrence of its name, in this case linking with the appearances
or biographies of a whole parade of lovers, so what she thinks of as human help from him
is no longer dependent on changing her desire for him in the present, but is a substitute for it.
The landscape is empty *and* it is immanent. The context of the woman in its reality
may be different from the context in which the viewer thinks about her, the element of transparency.
The way the viewer thinks about her is the way low clouds extend a landscape. The viewer
is acting on the landscape in consideration that the context of the viewer distinct from the context
of general human help could be a metaphor for itself.

There were yellow-leaved trees behind a screen of green ones at the edge of the orchard.
They are not a border between organization and decay of autumn trees, which are organized.
The yellow leaves around your feet have an impossible beauty that was achieved and then lost.
A way you can define a woman is to remember everything the woman is not.
If you move your head fast enough, you can all of a sudden discern the whole structure
of the surface of each leaf, and it links in your stomach, as with sex.
If you remember not desiring her fast enough, you can all of a sudden discern her whole body,
and you can feel it in your stomach, the way any moment that happened and in which you think about
    her goes
a long way toward convincing you of the autonomy and pre-existence of her form.

3

Her concentration became a direct experience of his life, an erotic concentration.
Her biography of her persistently locates the point of impact of one's own system of representations,
insofar as vision itself is a representative operating on what she sees,
and for which a particular light can represent an initial condition. Even the slightest movement
of a hand or a finger is controlled and emphasized as by a spotlight of this sensitiveness,
the way repetition is a cessation of the potential for conscious experience, or death,
visiting the same places during the same seasons, at almost the same hour,
so that landscape could be a simple repetition which thrives on reproduction,
in order to resolve what is happening into its own combination or name of words in the form of its time,
and in order to defer the story.

In a way, her memory is a theory about how the hanged woman looked to her in the orchard
which she has to respect, in the sense that the landscape's immanence is an organically developing
failure of its language to speak its content. The connection between word and idea corresponding

to the landscape is retained, but the connection between the word and the landscape is lost,
so the shadow of a hill stays dark during lightning. How she sees the lightning
is a time-lapse into the planar dimension, a hierarchy of grammar or deference
by way of the word belonging to her such as lady suicide or woman suicide,
because the woman doesn't die in her own absence or in effigy, so that
no existing philosophy and no philosopher will know soon, enough points with enough speed
to handle the richness of her reconstruction of her or him for long. He starts to see
patterns in the words and the patterns are pretty to him and distract him.

It is well known that lightning is attracted to body heat, a person on horseback
or a large saguaro, the way a racket of birds in the morning is a kind of empathy for two people.
If we retain the belief that her image of him or her, let's say him, is a prerequisite for
gaining consciousness of the unknown person, we suppose there is no direct channel of communication
to the unknown person, with the result that facts about him or her must exit into the world
before a life can be perceived between the light and dark of function or the object, and desire or the image.
At any time one can turn into its opposite, like desire or a screen, and the object
or her story and him, who does not so much convey an image as a background
to the biography. So, he says, she must emphasize references and conditions of her own life
over its memories or what she sees of the landscape by the manner of its illumination,
unless she says it is illuminated within the limbs of a great cottonwood, yellow or green,
a faith of imaginary or real connotation repeating itself from him, like alternating current
or radioactive dirt being turned up that registers on her without marking her.

4

Her persistent observation, even after the frost, is of each leaf coinciding with its luminousness,
because of its structure as a lighted space and which shows brightness in idea and form,

so you have to maintain your own consciousness in order not to be unconscious with me.
Even if we can uniquely bridge the gap between the fact of a frost and the value
of luminousness, and even though these intrinsic properties of the plant may not be what it feels.
What it feels may be a space with pillars, so that with light the space extends, as in what you believe
to live with. A belief is a word-like object. You can focus your attention on it down to a point,
like desire or memory of a strong feeling. You have a certain amount of control over your feeling
about general human help by changing what you believe, which embodies the memories
your speech is empowered to represent, she says.

Space is material, but seems to open up a beyond which is thought to defy material in its failure
to speak its content. It still cues this content by links or desires, as to a form of physical appearance.
To the extent that she can reconstruct a context or pornography in her body suitable for a hanged woman,
a contingency is being beaten back, critically. In the sense that events happening at the same time
are meaningful, though not connected, there are events which mean nothing, though there is something
        to mean.
This is an easy way to expect with desire from moment to moment, while the woman was hanging herself,
as if consistency and the quest for certainty were not emotional,
as when a person begins telling a story, leaves move.
He believed that when a life is valuable, there is further value when it is responded to
as valuable, but this could occur through evaluative judgment, without his attendant emotion.
The product is in one case consistent manners, in the other, beautiful manners.

Honeymoon

1

Though relations with oneself and with other people seem negotiated in terms secretly confirmed
by representation, her idea of the person's visibility was not susceptible to representation. No matter
how emphatically a person will control his demeanor, there will be perspectives she cannot foresee or
direct, because there is no assignable end to the depth of us to which representation can reach,
the way part of a circle can be just the memory of a depth. The surface inside its contour,
like the inside of a body emits more feeling than its surroundings, as if
the volume or capacity of relations would only refer to something inside, that I can't see,
that the other person and I keep getting in the way of, or things in the landscape while they are driving,
instead of the capacity being *of* your person. The brightness of a cottonwood could be almost
a lack of volume or a lack of space inside the tree, the way a membrane is the entrance of an organism.
Here the person and the yellow tree would resemble the flesh of yellow fruit.

There are dimensions of an assessment of human relations, which go before and after our relation to
    the picture
as allegorical to what the picture is of, to what she sees or says about you as what her attachment to you
is *of*, so the narrow shadow of a cloud on a red cliff may just mark the plane of a line of print across
what you see, that could represent a perspective, as if some particular part were not turned toward you,
the way a fold can become a particular object or seam, like relations with oneself
or with another person. The fold is the shadow of a heavy eyelid on a cheek. My feeling for it
is like the flash in the rearview mirror of a pickup as I pass it in the dark,
my fixation on *my* body's opacity.

2

If the tree is yellow in the fall in mercury light by the river, I feel it gather its color
from the river. An orange moon is partially hidden in clouds in the darkness. Whenever
or wherever it is possible to speak of recognition, there was a prior hiddenness or border of the circle.
It's like driving without headlights on the plain, the moon's appearance as a lake by a power plant, a dead lake,
whose color neither hides nor doesn't hide a perspective. I would call it color, if the way
the texture of skin on his hand changes in moonlight were a color, instead of a fantasy,
so that the physical idea of his privacy is not made clearer by the idea of his secrecy.
It is the same sentence as trying to explain how her assessment could not wait for her uncertainty,
the arc of a head turning away from her over a shoulder, in autumn light,
sky filling with plausible though speculative bodies of light.

A yellow cottonwood in glory by a river on the plain, mature and yellow.
A yellow apple could be a small hollow in stone of light that flows over and over.
When he thinks about capacity, or she thinks about volume, they are thinking at first about the inside, *an*
other to *an* other, who seem to be reference points. But out here in nature,
which we do not call thinking, concepts seem to exist before there are characters to fulfill them.
(The before is utter dark before a perception.)

3

Adjacent to the blue enamel edge of the door of a cabinet, she sees the long hole of a riverbed on the plain.
If she were at the bottom of this canyon, she would be hidden, *and* she would be private. During
the possibility of a red reflection of light on the wall in front of you, you can imagine yourself,
even wearing a red coat, to be private as a mood, or hiding behind something that is transparent,

which places you at a particular distance away. This distance is the beauty of the person in your memory,
held by what obscures it most, daring yourself to imagine the person as even more beautiful?
You would be hiding behind a pane of glass in the atmosphere, or an example inaccessible to what
you are hiding, as if the beauty of the person, during a daydream, may flash across your mind,
like an animal across the landscape, forcing an exclamation from you, when you may not remember
    its name.

4

She is not the name of a person, nor *there* of a place, but they are connected with names.
There is a way of traveling, by rotating an orientation, while she remains within herself.
He moves his hand across the shadow, and it tints delicate skin on the back of his hand. He
has a doll in his mind, on which he can predict what she will be feeling, as if he would not
touch the doll, until her actual feeling would make contact with the object of his thought.

Why science does not use a word like she or there, is why the hand cannot make a sharp edge in the sand.
The hollow his hand would make in bright sun, micaed, was the place where the wing of the person
would fold into itself, almost a shadow in skin. The fold is the object or resemblance
between the head turning over a shoulder, and the wing folding.
He touches her shoulder at the place where the wing would begin, while she is sleeping.
She can concentrate on the objects in the room, and his talking to her, but the context is of losing herself
in possibilities like vowels, or birds during a period of plastic song, in which syllables are repeated
or rehearsed over and over. The head turns and lays itself in a hollow of skin along the ribs,
like a color onto the back of his hand, which could be one of her own thoughts.

5

The doll can be his level of representation, the way good is a level, although love is not a level.
The person thinks evil is the blood in him. It is syntax about a potential. The touch
of coyote skin would sufficiently turn him into a mangy coyote, whereas
if an animal dies and decays, he could be present as a scavenger. Now, his evil attitude
would be responsible, pervading the atmosphere, like ambiguity before a conception, or
like the actions of the hearts of the people around you. You have the sense of the color of a cheek.
Your sense of the colors of a heart moving is the assessment of a turning point, that curves
over territory like an edge of light, or the oxygenation of an emotion bypassing the doll.
The fold of a river meanders within the plain, sometimes hidden, like terraces of pollen in grass.
They occur on the skin of his fingertips, instead of along fissures of your thinking,
reflecting the brightness of a line, without the *idea* of the line.

6

If one string line of a bone crosses another properly, an area of brightness or intensity is created,
so that a skeleton, because it was hidden, appears to have been exposed almost inadvertently,
in the stance of a young boy who had been extracting a splinter from his foot that was resting on his knee, his hands
grasping the delicate foot. He makes a seamless extension from the space of the canyon into her mind.
Does seeking a cause make a line tremble, an act of the eye and the light, so that a space
will not stretch so immovably, nor each rock place itself as individual?
There is some gap between these feelings, or between a feeling and an action to be taken.
Filling a gap is not the movement of a limb or wing of the doll.

7

During their third sunset, the atmosphere grew bright and palpable.
Imagine the hand, and the forefinger is red, and the second finger is black. Each of the joints of
the fingers are of specified colors, and parts of the palm. Then the veins and distinct tissues inside
the hand are colored within each concavity, and also enameled on each surface of each part of tissue,
which she cannot project, because the colors array without motive, or like seeds during a time-lapse.

This is how a seed would germinate *and* be free of its blood, as in a hive or a galaxy.
She could think of how these colors fade, of things placed in a human context, a snakeskin,
wasp paper the color of blue corn, so what she understands is that light replacing color
becomes a span, like a stick dipped into water that appears still, but is smooth current.
A vertical dimension of red lies on the wall or within the wall, the way he might loosely lay himself
upon his own blood.

The shadow is not hidden, and the hand is not hidden. Only a tint of the cliff
behind the hand would remind her of an impatience in him, the part of the body she can't see around,
disembodied, loose. But for all she knows, it is loose inside.

8

She has to get right the occasion for visualizing his concept of the doll, but she cannot. While
she cannot experience the meaning of his assessments about the doll, it seems rags to her. So
she has to justify her blindness to its hunger, for example. She would say, I think
she has eaten already. She would scatter crumbs on her own dress to prove this. But
this place in this light may just be a place you don't know, a route you both traveled after dark
to a north rim. You have a feeling of having traveled through the space, without recognizing it.
Not recognizing the doll would have to be something you both study, like a dead language.

She thinks his relations with his own mind may flash intuitions, which force him to pass over
any attempt to say anything to himself. Not as a child would throw a ball out of its crib, and you
would carry it back. He would like to pass something over to one side that does not come back.
How you look into the canyon, a relation to lit and unlit complexities of islands on the canyon floor,
is the complicated question of looking, and the right answer that comes back. The more
complicated the question, the less light would come back, until no light comes back.
You would know everything you see in the first place, but the terms of your recognition grow
increasingly intimate and ecological, like the light of the gold of jewelry on you, which
while it is still light, is still becoming abstract.

9

She may suppress or otherwise lose all memory of a dimension, and how it felt.
Then she would refer to it as if it were happening to someone else.
She would wish his wish was to illuminate her behavior by means of referring to what she is feeling,
in order to reach the same place her reference to herself occupies, that is, before
she would express the feeling. It is how a particular color would be the knowledge that
would come of the light of the color, like a source to see whiteness from, that would puff like clouds,
if she referred to them, or like a bar of light touching down at the edge of the road.
You see grass plants through the color, as if the ground were hidden behind a plane of the atmosphere,
the animal licking its foot. The delicate skin of its tattoo is wearing away.
She begins to acquire honeymoon as a level of representation, something which may call
an application of honey onto a bar of light, or the part of a deep orange moon that is hidden, then
not hidden by clouds, having a sense of, but no analysis of her seeing to explain
her feeling for an application, how the ambiguity *seems* to alter "how much" is seen.

10

A creature walks on the quiet floor of the canyon, a dry floor, sparking with mica, under which water flows,
and turns its head aside from a thorny bush with red seeds hanging down. The light is so bright,
its volume would be a source to see whiteness from, which falls on a hand or on jewelry differently.
If she walked to the edge of the canyon and looked down, the creature would pass twelve feet below.
Like an image it would absorb her interest, or like an oxygenation along the miles of the insides
of its living cells. The creature is a motive which could generate an image of her own body
disappearing and appearing again after an interval or length of the canyon.
This occurs center stage with footlights illuminating it, where she is the footlight.
She can trace paths through the space of a canyon, generating a motive of it which to light,
a case where there would be some way of applying the color, like some form of light projection,
saturating or fusing all the particles at all levels of the insides of the capacities.
It is how the ghost of an image was made to appear in his mind.
How deeply he can feel it is not a matter of what feeling "a reason" causes in him.

11

The human being, troubled by limits, creates a trip for herself, which recreates her
as spacious. Now, she projects expanse onto endeavors such as the representation of an angel,
or the way the colors of the world would lie over the world, a pleasurable collation of objects,
as of hues of the shadow of an emergence place.
It passes a richness of seeing or believing back onto the impasto of the colored things,
in which anyone else may mean anyone other than the two of us, or anyone other than you, and you will go,
who are the color of a seam, and not a doll
of painted bisque which makes matte protuberances or patches of invisible places across a space.
A cloud in the morning folds over a monument on the plain, a vector like an avalanche of mist concealing it.

She creates a dark flank of a mountain, a person's thoughts or feelings, passing across the person, concealing
the person.
She wonders what the body would reveal, if the cloud were transparent.
It pervades the creation of a motive, like the action of a heart.

Note for the Second Edition

It was the 80s.

I was living alone in northern New Mexico. A friend from Laguna Pueblo sent me Wittgenstein's *Remarks on Color*; a friend told me about John Ashbery's *Self-Portrait in a Convex Mirror*. There was the collage aesthetic of the postmodern. There was improvisation in dance and music. Appropriation. I started to feel my way toward an intuited subliminal wholeness of composition. I wrote from note to note, without thinking of form. I allowed emotion to glue sentence to sentence. I was exploring abstraction as lyric. I did not understand what I wrote.

A friend brought me to a party for *L=A=N=G=U=A=G=E* magazine; a friend sent me lectures of Lacan. I met Georgia O'Keeffe, Agnes Martin.

I taught poetry in Alaska.

I wanted to feminize scientific language and philosophic language. I wanted to diffuse polarities between emotion and thought, between image and discourse, representation and abstraction, material and immaterial.

Working with other artists was a way to experience social space, family. "Blue Taj" was a collaboration with artist Gordon Baldwin, who managed a bookstore in Taos, and later established the photography department at the Getty Institute. "Alakanak Break-Up" and "Fog" are texts for the choreography of Theodora Yoshikami and The Morita Dance Company. "Forms of Politeness" is my dialogue with a woman who hanged herself in an orchard near my parents' house in Maine. And "Honeymoon" was a collaboration with sculptor Richard Tuttle.

I was exploring how much one person can communicate with another, can know another.

My experience was natural light and the seasons of northern New Mexico. I internalized the high desert landscape. The slow arc of the sun across "empty" land became long, poetic lines.

—Mei-mei Berssenbrugge
2019

Acknowledgments

Grateful acknowledgment to *Bridge, Caliban, Conjunctions, Parnassus, Temblor,* and *Tyuonyi,* where some poems first appeared.

"Honeymoon" was first published in a different form as "Hiddenness" by the Whitney Museum Library Fellows.

Thank you, Basement Workshop, National Endowment for the Arts, New Mexico Arts Commission, Yaddo, and the city of Dillingham, Alaska.

Thank you, Station Hill Press and New Directions Publishing.